Susan Skinner (pseudonym Susan Holliday) is a writer, teacher, calligrapher and printmaker. She has published four collections of poetry and her poems have appeared in a number of magazines and anthologies. Her agent (not for poetry) is Lesley Pollinger of Paper Lion Ltd. who has enabled Susan to publish a number of children's novels.

She has had a wide career in education, ranging from art teacher in a hospital school to creative writing tutor and lecturer.

Susan has a big family as she and her husband took on her sister's four children when her sister died at a young age.

She has three children of her own, five grand-children and three great-grand-children.

She now lives in a very friendly village, alone with her inspiring but time-consuming dog, Alfie, who does not go for walks but sniff-along, giving his mistress time to write haikus in her head!

Susan has always been fascinated by the world about her, the people in all their complexity, the countryside's history and its natural beauty. She also finds reading a great solace and joy.

These poems are dedicated with love to my family.

Susan Skinner

LIGHT BEHIND THE SHADOWS

A collection of poems

AUSTIN MACAULEY PUBLISHERS™

LONDON • CAMBRIDGE • NEW YORK • SHARJAH

A CIP catalogue record for this title is available from the British Library.

ISBN 9781398442122 (Paperback)
ISBN 9781398442139 (ePub e-book)

www.austinmacauley.com

First Published 2023
Austin Macauley Publishers Ltd®
1 Canada Square
Canary Wharf
London
E14 5AA

I would like to thank all the friends I have who have always been a great support to me and those in the poetry world who have put me in the right poetic direction, especially Anne Clarke and Mandy Pannett. I would also like to thank Austin Macauley for their care and attention.

Table of Contents

Messages

Points of Gold

Star Tracks

Above the winter stars mark out
their tiny campsites in the dark.
Universes back they shine,
steadfast across emptiness.
They tell us to be unafraid,
to light a fire on this lonely
camping ground and face the shining track
of time who bears the starlight on his back.

For we may all hold up a star
beneath the sky's great company;
and watch its light, however small,
shine on life's confusing track.
And as we watch, these stars time has made old,
turn their raging fires to points of gold.

Winter Ways

I wonder, did you have a choice or not
confronted by two ways in the wood?
Do you recall a hare in flurrying snow

leaping down the path to where you stood,
rising on hind legs, its silky ears
upright, waiting, or the darkening brood

of shadows soundless as your hopes and fears,
silent as the fallen snow is silent
as the owl with feathers like white fires?

Do you recall where the corner bent
into an unknown place there was a sudden
flicker as a slab of snow that leant

half on, half off the branch sprayed the untrodden
ground with marks like symbols you could read?
Careful graffiti that gave way to sodden

crystal holes: were these an ancient creed
of nature begging you to take this path
as if your walking here was a wild need?

I wonder, did those gods force you to take
a path of white enchantment, hidden codes
to give you visions, keep you wide-awake?

Message

Will you come down? Night's a daisy field
of stars and you are ghost-like in the attic.
Your vigil's over – something strange and new
shines on the stairway – winter's lost its crown.

The moon rises from the attic roof,
Orion walks away, the dog sleeps,
head on pillow in the garage. Truth
has many faces, while this one weeps,

another smiles. Come down! The pale moon sends
a message through the skylight: Spring is here,
she treads the garden of the innocents –
primrose tulip crocus hellebore –

a trail of flowers beneath the stars in flight
come down wrapped gently in the folds of night.

Homeless

I cup your spirit in my hands,
it is a bird fallen from its nest,
its heart flutters
its beak opens and shuts.

In my garden, the jasmine tree
creates delicate white flowers,
bees cluster, honeysuckle trails
scents of summer.

The church clock points to here and now
cows amble
seagulls fly in from the sea
sheep eat grass.

I will place you in a shaft of gold,
the sun will melt your fear,
my garden turn your empty heart
into a home.

Far from Home

If you have been to Paradise,
the coming home is stony hard.
Winter winds bring loneliness,
for here is no celestial yard.

No angels guard the earthly gate,
hills bear a drifting mistiness,
stars shine with an alien light
if you have been to Paradise.

The Immigrant and the Tern

Little tern, give me your strength.
In thirty years, you fly so far,
your flights can only be compared
to going to the moon and back three times!

Give us your hope.
You return in spring to settle
in Arctic breeding grounds. Your nest
is like a bowl placed on the mottled ground.

Give us your courage:
The sea has warmed, the fish you need have gone.
Your breeding ground for centuries has changed
into a place of mass mortality.

Your little chicks are dying of starvation
and you, who danced to win your mate for life,
who guarded baby chicks with piercing cries,
leave their little bones lost in the nest

or tossed by Arctic winds like tiny twigs
or buried in the snow, anonymous.
Yet, Sterna Paradisae, who have suffered
as many suffer, *you* are not defeated.

But we are only human and stay here
unwinged and on our knees. Little tern,
from this place each night we watch the moon.
Do we see you there, urging us on?

Old Man

The old man, defaced, lost,
hoards a silent sorrow
under the bare trees
empty of birds – the cost
of a cold season.

He walks slowly, pushes
his life like a rusty pram.
'Get going, Jim, my lad,'
cries the runner hurrying by,
'or you won't make it today.'

'Or ever,' the old man thinks,
waving his crooked finger.
He remembers his father's clock,
its oak wood gleams and winks,
its ticking: start, stop, start.

That was before the fire
melted his face, before
he lost his world, and yet,
'I will not retire from life,

until,' he says, looking up
at the clear blue space
caught by the baize twigs,
'I have found the green temple,
the gentle place
that will give me peace.'

Gold

In an ageless interlude
– no wind no whispering rain –
he thought about gold,
how it carries the sun,
how it can weigh a man down.

Above him, caught in a tree's twig-web
delicate yellow leaves
captured the sun's thin rays
before they fell, fragile, sparse
on autumn's bronze ground.

Anything can happen now, he thought
maybe you will step frail and slow
as a yellow leaf, from behind the tree's wrought
trunk. The sun's gold will glow on you,
give you my long love's halo.

The Dance of Death

Here is the dance of death
Pope, prelate and king
Constable, steward, cleric
those who turn the soil
dance with skeletons
joining hands with the dead.
But there is no dance of death:

only a closing in
only a loneliness
as the daisy shuts its petals
at the fall of night
as its petals lose their white
and peel off one by one.

Le-Puy-En-Velay

High on a hill the old cathedral stands.
Medieval pilgrims came here to begin
their journey to St Jacques de Compostela.
Were their sins forgiven?

Today we climb the penitential steps.
High Mass: the English choir wear red. Waterfalls
of song echo from the ancient walls,
the organ's mighty sound rebounds against

high windows, heights of stone.
We listen as those gathered into time
once listened to the chant of many choirs.
And now the fragile bishop speaks of love.

Is it because he's sick he talks of love
or does he know that little word once touched
the pilgrim dead and that we too will wait
for love to wake the angel in our hearts?

At the End of the Day

At the end of the day,
I will pick up all my memories,
yes, all my memories,
however rough, however small.
I will spread them out over the kitchen table
then cup them in my hands; they are to me
more lovely and more real
than the red roses growing against the wall,
or the smiling moon wrapped in her great shawl
of starred indigo.

The night wind leaps
like a frog through the open window.
My memories will not blow away,
however small, however rough;
they are closer to me
than evening blackbirds, high, invisible,
whistling their madrigals.
Late at night, when dark on dark will fall,
I'll throw my memories up among the stars
to guide me as I go.

Grief

Rain taps the roof,
I climb the stairs,
I read messages on the landing
hidden in the carpet.
I draw the curtains
against invasive light.
This is a square
I will always honour.

At night the bed has doubled its size,
the alarm clock ticks – one hand
lodged at the bottom of time.
Books waiting to be read.

Once you told fortunes.
Here are your tarot cards,
The Popess, The Hanged Man
which will I hold?

From my window
the church clock strikes,
time scuttles under the carpet
like a mouse.

A bird sings.
Beside the roar of nameless traffic
a bird sings.
I must not forget that!

Weaving Time

Spring dips into a storm
trees break and fall
revealing twisted roots.
The once blue sky is grey,
indefinite.
Clouds like ghosts follow one another
to the horizon.

In June, the palace flakes in mid-day heat,
water trickles to a halt, my suitors
fight and shout in the antechamber

while I weave slowly, slowly in my sorrow.
Friends surround me, hide the greed and chaos.
At night, one lamp burns, a flickering moon-flake.

My suitors snore like pigs while we unravel
our weaving from the day before. The wool
lies in a maze of purple like bruised skin.

Each day I weep and every night I weep.
O man who is my anchor and my ship
in your great absence there is much to do.

Winter comes,
distorts images
of land and sea.
There's still no sign
of boat or flag. I sit
and watch the long horizon that divides us
year on year.

Nature

New Life

Tokens

Late September, sun spills in the east,
early dew glints like glass beads

on grass and leaves; the new sun brushes light
between stripped trees whose leaves are lifted

by the wind's gathering and drift down,
golden-brown, orange, yellow, purple,

onto the path. We walk the forest way
pick up leaves whose colours startle us,

put them in our pockets, ready to press,
bright tokens of a lost summer.

Garden Chair

A slab of light sits
alert, ready to fall
from the chair in the pebbled
corner of the wall.

Shadows sink
into the black holes of its back
woven from dried drift wood.
There's a tinge, a smack

of tar, wind-worn, sea-worn.
Light slips off the chair slowly
at a sharp angle, slides onto the ground.
The seat is empty.

Startled by a vision
I watch an old man glide
towards the seat
in a spangle of untied

silver and white. Is he unreal?
He whispers of the song
he sang for her when she sat there,
but she has gone.

Then he dissolves; only memory
that dark tenacious queen
sits in the empty chair
upright, unseen.

On a Bench

It's light weather, light on willow leaves
light dipped in streams, light in waves
of whispering grass,
light on bees' wings, passing butterflies.

I see you waiting, straw hat tilted, grave
yet jocular, sitting on the raised
bench above the grass and I gaze
hoping you will see me. For this day,

this minute is see-through, the light grazes,
reveals at the same time – the way
a mirror reflects – your face, my face,
the other side of light and loneliness.

Seascape at Dusk

Nothing is still.
Sky's evening colours dip,
orange, green, gold,
into the glassy waters that absorb
the sinking sun.

And when night comes,
silent as a petal falls
from flower to earth,
the moon silently falls into the sea.
Nothing is still.

The Leaf

Heart-shaped leaf
your veins hold the seasons.

Tender green, delicate,
Spring in their rising.

Flushed bronze in Autumn,
falling in Winter,

crushed in the snow,
passing a message

sacred and secret
to clusters of buds

that have come to replace you
whose veins hold the seasons…

Spider

A spider's web
patterns my window
its delicate weaving
hung with sun drops,

intimate, miniature
in its perfection.
An evening sun
squints behind it.

Night squares up.
Touching my window, the web sings
a silent sonata.

Birds in the Chapel

They flutter, feather on stone
winging their flight
through fluted arches,
clatter, pecking at glass.
Sunshine is their home, the green hills.

They cannot get out,
the window is iron-barred.
Are they the feathered ghosts
of Cathar refugees
who fled the Northern Knights
only to be killed?

Night is their resting place.
They fly to the rafters
settle, feather and heart
but when the window burns
with another day
they flutter feather on stone…

Leaf Talk

I said to the end of the world:
'You can't catch me.
I am an unfurled seed,
a wind will fly me
onto another earth
another tree.

I will blossom with spring birds;
they will hide me in their song.
Unseen I will unfurl
with their green growing leaves.'
I said to the end of the world: 'You can't catch me.'

Small Bird

I hold a small bird
fallen from its nest.
It flutters
opens and shuts its beak.

In my garden
the jasmine tree
streaks pink flowers
against the wall.

Wisteria bends and twists,
its blue tassels hang
in a bower of leaves.
Will you hide there?

The church clock points
to here and now,
cows amble, a white flare
of gulls flies in from the sea.

Sheep bend to grass,
sun anoints their backs.
The oak tree is stronger
than two hundred years.
Small bird, as days pass
maybe you will fly
up into the tree,
let the sky settle over you.

Stone

Modest, more ancient than our imagining
this stone lies silent in the earth
round and smooth and still,
not worn away

in the turning universe,
but noiselessly refined.
Does it remember its first flying
in fiery dark,

part of a mighty wing
falling, falling
before the shape of things
before birds sang

calling the sun to rise,
before clouds drifted, slow as cattle
below the stars
from where it first came?

Lockdown Garden
August 2020

My garden is a haven
for yellow-striped bees.
In the hot air
they buzz and murmur
round moss-green leaves
collecting nectar
from lavender sprays.

Here is a heaven
for butterflies.
This one flutters, lighter than light,
steps on a pink petal,
closes its wings as if in prayer
then opens them up in a chime of colour
and flies away.

Here is a hidden paradise
where even the sky sheds
blue petals of summer
and from the shining laurel
– a one bird choir –
is it a thrush?
sings to the day.

Night Owl

I am white owl, stars rain on me,
moon is my halo, I move wind-fast.
My vision is clear as the star that shines
between the twigs of my twisted oak.
My claws are sharp as ice and you,
who watch my feathers fall, know nothing
of what I know. My kingdom circles
yew, ash, chestnut. I lasso
stars with my far-flung wings; I am
the High White King of the dark forest.

The Walk

Serrated nettles curve down to the wayside
path where earth is interlocked, eroded.

Like a dull mosaic lying between
high banks, leaves, dried brown, mottled green

scuttle in the wind. Yet in the meadow
there are signs of new life: violets grow,

grass reveals shy buttercups whose hidden
leggy stems and stalks absorb in the sudden

rash of sunlight, the sun's yellow and gold
as if, petals uplifted, flowers hold

their own bright vision, and I conjure up
the childhood times when we picked buttercups

to test if we liked butter or plucked handfuls
of dock leaves to mellow the sting of nettles,

or the buttercup tree we once saw in the sun
with all its petals floating down and down.

Out of the blue, rain spikes the grass, winds blow.
Now I must leave the field and all its shadows.

Early Morning Over
the River Ouse

The sky opens out, embracing earth.
Silence.
I did not come prepared for silence.
I wait. From Hamsey Church sun sweeps across
trees, hedges, pastures.
A blackbird calls
telling the people to get up, to leave
their sorrow to the moon.

Now at daybreak
reeds sparkle like green swords
and the river
carrying light's broken jewellery
meanders, whispering
its wind chant,
its water song
its deeply flowing need to pour itself
into the open sea.

Before Daybreak

It is a quiet time:
The moon spills its ghosts over the grass.
A deer comes out of the wood soundlessly.

A star signals from its outpost
as if it is lonely up there
far from autumn bonfires,
the smell of wood smoke.

It is a still time
before daisies prize open
their white crowns
or foxgloves shiver.

The dark sky quivers to grey,
fallen leaves – bright embers of the year
bury the ground
in silent colours –

amber, bronze, crimson.
It is a time of acceptance:
dying leaves and small shoots lie
side by side.

Autumn Walk

A grey sky slumps
like an old raincoat. Four seagulls
rise from its pockets.

Chimneys smoke their grey
melancholic pipes, foursquare
over red-brick houses.

Below our feet
fallen copper leaves,
touched by shadows,

lie on their side,
their veins like needles
threaded by the sun.

We walk on,
our footsteps tread
green grass cities,

home to worms and ants
their egg-laying always
a bid for renewal.

Journeys

The Last Star

Time

He is gentle, intransigent,
he does not leave my side.
I watch the wind swivel
a paper bag, flap it round a post,
so Time's soundless breath
wraps me round.

Beyond a network of trees
the hill leans against
a grey sky, indigo clouds fly
like flocks of black-winged geese.
Now winter darkness drifts
along the path.

We walk hand in hand,
a star signs to us between branches.
I will never comprehend
why Time brought me here
or how he will lead me past
the last tree, the last star.

In the Dumps

January: on the far side of the street
pools of light glamorise shop sales,
line the road like carpets of gold silk.
Beyond the centre, roofs are stubborn grey
gaunt on a hill, trees spike the glowering sky.

This side, the thick walls of the dump are green
and people enter, day on day, heaving
burdens in their arms, their faces lined.
Only the operators smile, dividing
goods for resurrection and recycling:

throw-aways that line this underworld.
The path between four dumps is like the Styx
where what was bright and loved is stowed away,
shoved into steely pits and lost forever
underneath the earth. Yet still they come

all through the day in cars that carry outsize
wardrobes, carpets, mattresses, huge loads
high enough to clothe and house a city.
Only one man thinks again and keeps
a box of toys as if he knows its value

lies in itself. He carries it with care
walking away beyond the clamorous sales.
The day grows colder, a round shouldered sun
forces its way between the spiky trees
making a smudge of yellow like a sign.

Journey

He walked away from grief
left the gate open
fled into autumn's windfall –

bronze thud of apples,
creak of leaves,
the rise and fall
of wild migrating geese.

Trees groaned
briars bent double.
Her spirit blew him seaward.

He took a boat and sailed into winter.
In France the evening light was lost
in rhythms of snow.
The sun flew to its nest.

Only the sweeping grey of coming night
clothed the sky.
Light unbuckled.

Silence, save for her voice.
Trees hid the horizon
A threadbare sky
let through the snow.

From the bleak north
he travelled south,
guided by her spirit,

past half-way snowdrops,
into the green breath
of another Spring.
In Ravello his heart stood still.

Here he would lie her down
in peace and make
good the greenways of his broken heart.

Wondering

At the edge of the wood
a landslide of shadows
buries the sun

I think of your childhood
summers of blue
breaking through leaves

when buttercups stood
like a hundred kings
cupping the sun

when in the void
of a fairy ring
you waited, wondering.

I wonder, subdued,
if I should stay
in this light, these colours,

or walk in the wood
to touch its darkness
to lose my fear.

At the edge of the wood
a landslide of shadows
buries the sun.

The Pink Moon
For Peter

He wandered out into the Spring night,
flowers closed their petals
silently.

The glory of the sky
beckoned him
to walk from star to star.

Lower down a clear-cut moon
scudded in and out
of wispy clouds.

It shone on him,
it followed him.
'The pink moon,' he cried.

The pink moon's call was clear –
to venture to the place
beyond its light, beyond the stars.
He thought about his child,
the apple of his eye,

her brothers whom
he had made his own,
their mother
whom he loved.

Would they grieve
that they were of the earth
and he the sky?

On that Spring night
he walked and walked alone
beyond the moon.

Winter

It is frost time
no red leaves hang
or flowers flame,

stars break the sky in depths
of dark and light
slowly the camels walk

towards the round dome
that is pointing upwards.
Bells chant and chant.

The world stands still to listen
it is the white time,
hope is not lost.

Who Are You?

You come from stardust
bathe in sea water
fear the cliff's edge.

Each time you question
your very existence
your moods swing

from moon to sun.
You harvest the world
on mountain tops,

in petals, in forests,
in the buzz of a bee;
you too collect honey.

Sometimes you run away,
turn to the city,
drown in its noise.

Tell me, what landscape
embraces you, gives you a place to stand up in,
to eat, to dance in,
to learn life's times table
to know you are home?

The Refugee's Arrival

Hollow and huge waves
close in on the children
– tumbling into the sea –
yet even here
in the cries and shrieks
of a fallen world,

even in the sea's rage
and his only child drowned,
his grief deeper than drowning,
his future torn,
even here on this unknown beach,
he hears you.

On this foreign beach, he hears you:
not like the wind swinging
from bough to bough
or blackbirds trilling,
not like the cry
of gulls sharp and piercing,

but like the sound of a flame;
not a candle
waving and whispering
round its dark centre
or a fire crackling
into the night sky

but the flame of Easter faith
that sometimes but not often
enters God's domain.
So he stands up,
the bewildered refugee,
and walks this unknown land.

How Will You Travel?

How will you travel? In a sailing ship
that leaves a troubled sea for the horizon,
where light skies and seagulls slide and slip

into an evening sea and gold rays tip
the waves and then weave downward, finely spun?
How will you travel? In a sailing ship?

Or like a humming bird that longs to sip
from the exotic flowers it rests upon,
where light skies and white seagulls slide and slip?

Your journey is a long unfailing trip
to reach the yellow petals of the sun.
How will you travel? In a sailing ship?

You'll watch the sea and sky fold lip to lip
like shining lovers when their love is won
where light skies and white seagulls slide and slip

until sun's fiery colours dive and dip.
Then you will travel in the dark, alone,
where no skies light, no seagulls slide and slip.

Change

This river has a long history
of flowing downward
from the mountain stream
towards this place of change
where fresh water
slides into the sand
yellow and crushed and changeable. Here tides
ride back and forward like a green mosaic
of fish and sunlight.

And now, like the river,
you are swamped,
you have no hold,
sea and storms confuse you.
Your well-known childhood landscape is subsumed,
and it is a hard
to tread this wide sea
to the other side.

Travelling Home

As I travel home on the Bakerloo Line
I think there is no love
so long, so lasting
as a mother's for a child.

I am heady with last night's Messiah,
its cadencies of praise
and I wonder if God's love
is longer, more lasting.

Some love is lyrically imposed:
it dances on our eyelids,
dips in and out of green leaves
then becomes the shadow, not the sun.

And I cannot really speak for God
only for this different love I feel
as I travel home on the Bakerloo Line
while other passengers sit

in upright silence and a young man
is fast asleep on a priority seat

and two girls wear bright red lipstick
and very short skirts. Maybe they are twins,
maybe they are longing for love,
maybe – but I can only think there is nothing
so long, so lasting as a mother's love for a child.

Arrival

Beneath the ferry
the sea dives like a shoal of dark blue dolphins.
Rain spindles down.
You say, soon our dreams will dissipate.

We talk of images of where we've been:
a French Abbey bathed in sunshine,
a modern church to Joan of Arc.
You say, history is memory in disguise.

Our country looks fragile:
white, crumbling cliffs barely hold up
against the sea's persistent breathing.
You say, one day the sea will cover this island.

Slowly we enter the harbour,
land takes on substance,
houses, roads, lampposts are in place.
You say, soon there will be a drowning.

In the ship's cavern cars roar to leave
like cows waiting to be released
from winter sheds into the sunshine.
I say, the light is still with us.

Song

I have come a long way.
Grasses whisper to me,
the sun livens my heart.

In autumn apples dropped in sorrow,
today their blossom clusters,
each fragile petal
bears a future.

I have come a long way.
In winter the earth curled up,
now it breaks open
to daisies, buttercups.

The house sparrow tweets
from a hole in the tile,
a straw in its mouth.
I have come a long way.

Costa Concordia

Many hands made me
sent me into the sea
a giant on tiptoe
dancing on waves.

I did not crave
to be like the Titanic,
I was bigger, safer,
I gathered

four thousand people into my arms.
I was forty hotels in one
I rode the sea's way
balancing glasses on a hundred trays.

I could withstand
The gale's molten anger,
the sun fragmenting,
sinking into the waves,

but not ice or rock,
not the miscalculation
that turned my island salute
into my death knell.

Now I lie beneath the sea.
Dreadnoughts of seaweed
blanket cabins,
bodies float through dark green corridors.

Paint Words Love

Gateways

To Rothco

Whose paintings are gateways
to those still waters
where we observe reflections
of ourselves, subtle dislocations
disturbances of paint
that catch the tail coat of a fear
always running away.

Was it these shapes,
these tragic presences,
colours feathered one against another
that fuelled your desire for death?
Or was it the loss
Of the time when you had no money
defied the terrible speed that ripped America?

Paint proposes a silent connection
to human feelings
and today our hearts live
in the strange, stretched square
of muted paint
unravelling from your heart.

The Bridge

We cross the bridge
below the Avon
talks to itself
swans gather for sleep.

Dusk throws to the water
her soft pink clouds.
We reach the other side.
Here, long ago

he carried his small son
deep in his heart,

bridged the whole world
with words of grief.

We imagine him walking
beside the river,
watching its shadows, thinking
we are all shadows.

Response to
Shakespeare's Sonnet 31

I have no means to follow where they go.
The road's unknown, I do not know the way.
Tall mountains cut the sky and there is snow.
I have no means to follow them today.

And even if that road was lined with flowers
whose colours claimed the radiance of the sun,
and even if my heart had unknown powers,
I could not follow where my loves have gone.

Yet I have not lost hope. I won't forget
those who have crossed the mountain for I have
memories, warm and secret in my heart
that like a nest holds them in my love.

And in my heart of hearts I know it's true:
all those I love have led me to love you.

Response to
Shakespeare's Sonnet 18

Were you to ask me why I read this poem,
I'd speak of last and lasting things: of day
and night dancing on earth's rim,
stones that wait in silence and the grey

thin cry of gulls across the marsh. I'd tell
of begging tunes men played and old gods spun
gathering music in a cosmic shell,
and though today tower blocks fall and flame

black figures leap onto the air and Vulcan's
hammer blows crack open little towns,
swirling waves mount up and up and drown
landscapes that have turned into a dream,

lost in the fury of the world, I'd say
this poem is the one that gets away.

The Seine at Asnieres

In a narrow orange rowing boat
a girl holds the oars, her long black hair
tied beneath a bonnet. Opposite,
her fair-haired friend
sits quietly and reads.
Round the boat sky-reflections quiver
silently, but as we look, we hear

water dripping, oars floating and diving
into the river, sunlit specks
shaking slivers of sky
into the Seine,
and though we note a house
still as its stone
beyond the distant shore,

we listen to the river flow and flow,
rolling towards us
almost touching us,
as if the scene was painted
with the feather
of some small bird
flying from then to now.

Afternoon Skyscape

Early afternoon, clouds jostle
in a lively blue sky.
A last whistle, then birds are still
and I lie on my back in the grass
wondering where you are.
Soon the world disappears

in a rustle of air, in the soft
white clouds that spill
over the blue.
And I think you are up there,
riding a cloud, passing by
to ease my grieving heart.

On Visiting Lascaux

Here are no tides to enthral time,
pull it into new seasons, unlock
sun and moon. Only darkness –
a bird whose huge black wings block
light – hides the marvellous still flights
of silent painted animals on rock.

What is the secret of your long silence,
deer, horse, mammoth painted deep
under the rocky earth? What is your silence?
It is night, you seem to say, *with no stars, sleep
with no dreams, it is the falling gap
between cliff and river when we leap*

or are made to leap into the unknown.
We too have silent treasure hidden
deep in the mystery of body and mind:
a song, a touch, an image that comes unbidden,
rare as a desert flower, briefly waking
an archaic meaning, then closing up again.

Mountainscape at Dawn

Night gathers up its stars, a ragged moon
hovers on the mountain top where dawn's
pale light turns half gold in the rising sun.

Lower down a fog hides a lost chapel,
a ruin except for the bell tower and bell
a shepherd rings each day as a memorial

for his dead family. A passing eagle
listens to the sad notes as they toll,
listens to their lonely mountain call.

The shepherd waits a while until the sun
burns off the fog then he walks down and down
back to the village house where he was born.

At First Sight

When I first met Alfie, it was night.
He lay on my bed shivering, legs up,
ears awry, tail a tawny brush.
At this third rescue
his submissive soul
held on tight
as if the still quiet and the stars
would make him whole.

I could not sleep, my thoughts were dark.
Was he dead or was he gathering up
the will to start again?
How could I tell this small unkempt dog
with runny ears
and matted hair
would make my heart once more
grow warm, grow light?

This Is Love

Gentle as green sap rising
to shapes and colours of Spring
allowing a wasted world
to find itself again.

Strong as a tall mountain
over a shallow plain
never losing its lordship
though many years have gone.

Constant as stars that gleam
at night and will return
though clouds and tempests build
a starless cabin.

December Night at the Stable

Moon silence, horse silence:
she limps in pain to reach
her net of hay.
Inside the row of stables others shift,
turn their soulful eyes

to the girl running towards her own horse.
Time passes. Now
through trees with crooked limbs
a round moon cartwheels, sending
a beam of white light onto the roof

of the stable where the girl
whispers into the horse's twitching ear:
'It will soon be better.'
She lifts the damaged hoof,
washes and binds the wound.

Night batters grey-black wings across the moon,
stable lamps go out
but the girl stays and whispers comfort things
to her horse. In the aloof, starless dark
only her love is light.